The Cross
AND THE
Beatitudes

Other Books by Fulton J. Sheen

Characters of the Passion

From the Angel's Blackboard

In the Fullness of Time

Lift Up Your Heart

Peace of Soul

Simple Truths

Seven Words of Jesus and Mary

Advent & Christmas With Fulton J. Sheen

Lent & Easter Wisdom From Fulton J. Sheen

The Cross
AND THE
Beatitudes

LESSONS
on
LOVE
and
FORGIVENESS

FULTON J. SHEEN

LIGUORI/TRIUMPH
LIGUORI, MISSOURI

Published by Liguori/Triumph
An imprint of Liguori Publications
Liguori, Missouri
www.liguori.org

Library of Congress Cataloging-in-Publication Data

Sheen, Fulton J. (Fulton John), 1895–1979
    The Cross and the Beatitudes : lessons on love and forgiveness /
Fulton J. Sheen.
        p. cm.
    ISBN 978-0-7648-0592-9 (pbk)
    1. Jesus Christ—Seven last words—Sermons. 2. Beatitudes—
Sermons. 3. Catholic Church—Sermons. 4. Sermons, American. I.
Title.
BT456.S44   2000
232.96'35—dc21   99–056416

Liguori Publications, a nonprofit corporation, is an apostolate of the
Redemptorists. To learn more about the Redemptorist Congregation,
visit *Redemptorists.com.*

Printed in the United States of America
09 08 07   10 9 8

Originally published in 1937 by P. J. Kenedy & Sons.
This edition copyright 2000.
This edition published by special arrangement with the Estate of
Fulton J. Sheen.

Dedicated
to
OUR HEAVENLY MOTHER
who
Through the Cross
Leads us to Beatitude

Contents

Foreword

This little book is a correlation of the Seven Beatitudes and the Seven Last Words. The eighth beatitude, in the language of Saint Thomas Aquinas, "is a confirmation and a declaration of all those that precede. Because from the very fact that a man is confirmed in poverty of spirit, meekness, and the rest, it follows that no persecution will induce him to renounce them. Hence the eighth beatitude corresponds in a way to all the preceding seven."

Though there is no strict correspondence between the Seven Beatitudes and the Seven Words, this work assumes they are not unrelated; in fact, each seems to be related to the other as precept and deed. Both were delivered on a mountain—Our Lord began his public life on the Mount of the Beatitudes and closed it on the Mount of Calvary. This books tells the story of how he practiced the meekness, the mercy, and the poverty of the Beatitudes. If it brings just one soul closer to Our Lord and his Blessed Mother it will have been eminently worthwhile.

CHAPTER ONE

❀

The First Word: The Lesson of Meekness

Blessed are the meek:
for they shall
possess the land.

Father, forgive them,
for they know not
what they do.

Our Blessed Lord began his public life on the Mount of the Beatitudes, by preaching: "Blessed are the meek: for they shall possess the land." He finished his public life on the Hill of Calvary by practicing that meekness: "Father, forgive them, for they know not what they do."

How different this is from the beatitude of the world! The world blesses not the meek, but the vindictive; it praises not the one who turns the other cheek, but the one who renders evil for evil; it exalts not the humble, but the aggressive. Social and political forces have carried that spirit of violence, struggle for power, and the clenched fist to an extreme the like of which the world before has never seen.

To correct such a warlike attitude of the clenched fist, Our Lord both preached and practiced meekness. He preached it in those memorable words that continue the Beatitudes:

> You have heard that it has been said: An eye for an eye, and a tooth for a tooth. But I say to you not to resist evil: but if one strikes you on your right cheek, turn to him also the other: and if a man will contend with you in judgment, and take away your coat, let go your cloak also unto him. And whosoever shall force you one mile, go with him two....You have heard that it has been said: You

shall love your neighbor, and hate your enemy. But I say to you: Love your enemies: do good to them that hate you: and pray for them that persecute and calumniate you that you may be the children of your Father who is in heaven, who makes His sun to rise upon the good and bad, and rains upon the just and the unjust. For if you love them that love you, what reward shall you have? Do not even the publicans do this? And if you salute your brethren only, what do you more? Do not also the heathens this? Be you therefore perfect, as also your heavenly Father is perfect.

But he not only preached meekness; he *practiced* it. When his own people picked up stones to throw at him, he threw none back in return; when his fellow townsmen brought him to the brow of the hill to cast him over the precipice, he walked through their midst unharmed; when the soldier struck him with a mailed fist, and made the Savior feel by anticipation the clenched fist of Communism he answered meekly: "If I have spoken evil, give testimony of the evil: but if well, why do you strike me?"

When they swore to kill him, he did not use his power to strike dead even a single enemy; and now on the Cross, meekness reaches its peak, when to those who dig into the hands that feed the world, and to those who pierce the feet that shepherd souls, He pleads: "Father, forgive them, for they know not what they do."

Which is right—the violence of Communism or the meekness of Christ? Violence says meekness is weakness. But that is because it does not understand the meaning of Christian meekness. Meekness is not cowardice; meekness is not an easy-going temperament, sluggish, and hard to arouse; meekness is not a spineless passivity that allows everyone to walk over us. No! Meekness is self-possession. That is why the reward of meekness is possession [of the earth].

A weak person can never be meek, because he is never self-possessed; meekness is the virtue that controls the combative, violent, and pugnacious powers of our nature, and is therefore the best and noblest road to self-realization.

The meek person is not one who refuses to fight, nor someone who will never become angry. A meek person is someone who will never do one thing: he will never fight when his conceit is attacked, but only when a principle is at stake. And there is the keynote to the difference of the anger of the violent and the anger of the meek person.

Communism begins at the moment conceit is attacked; fists clench and rise as soon as the ego is challenged; cheeks flush as soon as self-love is wounded, and blood boils and flows at that split second when pride is humbled.

The anger of the Communist or violent person is based on selfishness; he hates the rich not because he loves the poor in spirit, but because he wants to be rich himself.

He is really a capitalist without any cash in his pockets. Selfishness is the world's greatest sin; that is why the world hates those who hate it, why it is jealous of those who have more; why it is envious of those who do more; why it dislikes those who refuse to flatter, and why it scorns those who tell us the truth about ourselves; its whole life is inspired by the egotistical, the personal, and its wrath is born of that self-love.

Now consider the anger of the meek man. For the meek man, not selfishness but righteousness is his guiding principle. He is so possessed, he never allows his fists to go up for an unholy purpose, or in defense of his pride or vanity, or conceit, or because he wants the wealth of another. Only the principles of God's righteousness arouse a meek person. Moses was meek, but he broke the tablets of stone when he found his people were disobeying God.

Our Lord is Meekness itself, and yet he drove the buyers and sellers from the Temple when they prostituted his Father's House; but when he came to the doves, he was so self-possessed he gently released them from the cages. He is so much master of himself, that he is angry only when holiness is attacked, but never when his Person is attacked. That is why when the Gerasenes beseeched Our Lord to leave their coasts, without a single retort, "entering into a boat, He passed over the water and came into His own city."

That is why when men laughed him to scorn he said nothing but approached the dead daughter of Jairus and went on with his work of mercy, oblivious to their insults, and restored her to life. That is why he addressed Judas as "friend" when he blistered his lips with a kiss. That is why Our Lord from the Cross prays for the forgiveness of his enemies. Their wrath directed against his Body he would not return, though he might have smitten them all dead by the power of his Divinity. Rather, he forgave them, for "they know not what they do."

If ever innocence had a right to protest against injustice, it was in the case of Our Lord. And yet he extends pardon. Their insults to his Person, he ignores. Had he not preached meekness? Now must he not practice it?

And how could he practice it better than to pray for those who were crucifying him? And what greater meekness could there be than to excuse them because they knew not what they did. What a lesson for us to remember: that those who do us harm, may, too, be of the same type of misguided consciences as those who crucified Christ.

From that dread day forward, there have been two motives for withdrawing from battle: either because we are afraid or because we are husbanding our energies for a more important battle. The second kind is the meekness of Our Lord. Be not angry, then, when your conceit is attacked. It will do no harm. As Our Lord reminds us: "Blessed are they that suffer persecution for justice's sake; for theirs is the kingdom of heaven."

In contrast to this Christian philosophy of forgiveness, there exist in the world systems of philosophy and social and political structures based not on love, but on hate and greed. Communism, for instance, believes that the only way it can establish itself is by inciting revolution, class struggle, and violence. Hence its regime is characterized by a hatred of those who believe the family is the basic unit of society. The very communistic gesture of the clenched fist is a token of its pugnacious and destructive spirit, and a striking contrast indeed to the nailed hand of the Savior pleading forgiveness for the clenched-fisted generation who sent him to the Cross.

It is startling indeed to recall that we followers of Our Lord believe in violence just as much as do others of more obvious destructive intent. Has not Our Lord said: "The kingdom of heaven suffers violence, and the violent bear it away." But here is the difference: We do not believe in violence to one's neighbor; we believe in violence to ourselves. While Communists struggled against all who refused to have the same hate, we have struggled against ourselves, our lower passions, our concupiscences, our selfishness, our egotism, our sensuality, our meanness—in a word, against everything that prevents us from realizing the best and highest things in our nature. We do not crucify our enemies; we crucify that which makes us think anyone is our enemy. We Christians have love; we hate that which makes us hate our enemies. If the power-hungry, the godless, and the violent used as much violence on their selfishness as they use on others, they would all be saints!

Their hatred is weakness, for it refuses to see that collective selfishness is just as wrong as individual selfishness; it is the weakness of the man who is not self-possessed, who uses his fist instead of his mind, who resorts to violence for the same reason the ignorant man resorts to blasphemy; namely, because he has not sufficient intellectual strength to express himself otherwise.

What, then, must be our attitude toward the hatred shown to us? It must be the attitude of the Holy Father who asked us to pray for our enemies. It must be the attitude of those Spanish priests who before being shot by their persecutors asked them to kneel down and receive their blessing and their forgiveness. And what is this but a reflection of Our Lord's attitude on the Cross: meekness, love, and forgiveness?

What must be our attitude toward the evils of the world? We must possess a strength, a force, and a daring that exposes its errors and goes down to death on the Cross rather than accept the least of its principles of hate.

We will not be loved for our meekness, and it will be hard for us not to be angry when our conceit and our pride, and possibly our possessions, are attacked; but there is no escaping the Divine injunction: "Blessed are you when they shall revile you, and persecute you, and speak all that is evil against you, untruly, for my sake: Be glad and rejoice for your reward is very great in heaven"; and "If the world hate you, know you that it has hated me before you. If you had been of the world, the world would love its own; but because you are not of the world, but I have chosen you out of the world, therefore the world hates you"; and "The hour cometh that whosoever kills you will think that he does a service to God."

If then we have enemies, let us forgive them. If we suffer unjustly, then we can practice the virtue of charity. If we suffer justly, and we probably do, for we have sins to atone for, then we can practice the virtue of justice.

What right have we to hate others, since our own selfishness is often the cause of their hatred. The first word from the Cross and the Beatitude of meekness both demand that we tear up self-love by the roots; love our executioners; forgive them, for they know not what they do; do a favor for those who insult us; be kind to the thieves who accuse us of theft; be forgiving to liars who denounce us for lying; be charitable to the adulterers who charge us with impurity.

Be glad and rejoice for their hate. It will harm only our pride, not our character; it will cauterize our conceit, but not blemish our soul—for the very insult of the world is the consecration of our goodness.

We know it is not the worldly thing to do—to pray for those who nail us to a cross. But that is just the point: Christianity is not worldliness; it is turning the world upside down. We know it is not "common sense" to love our enemies, for to love our enemies means hating ourselves; but that is the meaning of Christianity—hating that which is hateful in us, and loving others because they are the potential children of God.

Often our enemy is our savior; our persecutor is often our redeemer; our executioners are often our allies; our crucifiers are often our benefactors—for they reveal what is selfish, base, conceited, and ignoble in us. But we must not hate them for that. To hate them for hating us is weakness. If we go on answering hate with hate, how will hate ever end? Answering violence with violence is to propagate further violence; strife increases the sum of bitterness, regardless of who triumphs. Hate is like a seed: if we sow it we reap more hate. If hatred is to be overcome, the sting must be taken out of it; it must not be nourished, or cultivated, or propagated. But how can this be, except by returning good for evil?

How else can we banish hatred from the earth? Suppose five thousand men are in line and before them is a demagogue and leader telling them that the only way they can overthrow governments and acquire property is by violence, revolution, and the clenched fist. Suppose the first man in line, inspired by that leader's hatred and propaganda, strikes the second man in line on the right cheek; the second raises his clenched fist to strike the third; the third wishes to strike the right cheek of the fourth, and on and on clenched fists fly—because their Gospel is hate.

Is there any way at all to stop that hatred and violence? Yes, on one condition, and that is if one man in that line who is struck on his right cheek, instead of striking his neighbor, turns and offers to the one who struck him his left cheek. He would kill hatred, because he refused to sow it. Hatred would no longer have soil on which it could grow, for hatred can grow on a right cheek but never on a left cheek: "If anyone strikes you on the right cheek, turn the other cheek." That is not weakness; it is strength—the strength that makes us masters of ourselves and the conquerors of hate.

If you doubt it, try it some time to see how much strength it takes. It took so much strength that only Divinity's cry of forgiveness could overcome the hatred of those who crucify.

If you have enemies, if they hate you, if they revile you, and persecute you and say all manner of evil things against you, and you wish to stop their hatred, to release the hatred in their clenched fists, drive them off the face of the earth—then there is but one way to do it: *Love them*!

❦

I saw the Conquerors riding by
With cruel lip and faces wan:
Musing on kingdoms sacked and burned
There rode the Mongol Genghis Khan;

And Alexander, like a God,
Who sought to weld the world in one:
And Caesar with his laurel wreath;

And leading, like a star the van,
Heedless of upstretched arm and groan,
Inscrutable Napoleon went
Dreaming of empire and alone....

Then all perished from the earth
As fleeting shadows from a glass,
And, conquering down the centuries,
Came Christ, the Swordless, on an ass?
—HARRY KEMP

CHAPTER TWO

❀

The Second Word:
The Lesson
of Mercy

*Blessed are the merciful:
for they shall
obtain mercy.*

*This day you shall
be with me
in paradise.*

At the beginning of his public life, on the Hill of the Beatitudes, Our Lord preached: "Blessed are the merciful: for they shall obtain mercy." At the end of his public life, on the Hill of Calvary, he practiced that Beatitude as he addressed the thief: "This day you shall be with me in paradise."

The beatitude of the world is quite different; it runs like this: "Blessed is the man who thinks first about himself." Life for the world is a struggle for existence in which victory belongs only to the egotists. Liberality, generosity, and graciousness are rare. How often the world insists on "rights," how rarely does it emphasize "duties"; how often it uses the possessive "mine," and how rarely the generous "thine." How full it is of "courts of justice," but how few are its "courts of mercy."

Our Lord came to correct such an exaggerated justice which knew no mercy. Mercy, he reminded us, was something more than a sentimental, emotional tenderheartedness. The very word mercy is derived from the Latin *miserum cor*, a sorrowful heart. Mercy is, therefore, a compassionate understanding of another's unhappiness.

A person is merciful when he feels the sorrow and misery of another as if it were his own. Disliking misery and unhappiness, the merciful person seeks to dispel the misery of his neighbor just as much as he would if the misery were his own. That is why, whenever mercy is confronted not only with pain, but with sin and wrong-doing, it becomes forgiveness which not merely pardons, but even rebuilds into justice, repentance, and love.

Mercy is one of the dominant notes in the preaching of Our Lord. His parables were parables of mercy. Take for example the hundred sheep, the ten pieces of money, and the two sons. Of the hundred sheep, one was lost; of the ten pieces of money, one was lost; of the two sons, one led a life of dissipation.

It is interesting to note that the lost sheep is the one that was sought, and the shepherd finding it, places it upon his shoulders and brings it into the house rejoicing. But there is no record in the Gospels of any such attention being paid to the ninety-nine sheep who were not lost.

When the woman lost a piece of money and found it, she called in her neighbors to rejoice. But there is no record that she ever called in her neighbors to rejoice in the possession of the other nine that were never lost.

One son went into a foreign country and wasted his substance living riotously. And when he came back, he was given the fatted calf. But the brother who stayed at home was not so rewarded. All these illustrations Our Lord followed with the simple truth: "There shall be more joy in heaven upon one sinner that does penance than upon ninety-nine just who need not do penance."

One day Peter went to Jesus to inquire just what limitation should be placed upon mercy. He asked Our Lord a question about mercy and gave what he thought was rather an extravagant limit: "How often shall my brother offend against me, and I forgive him? Till seven times?" And Our Lord answered, "Not till seven times, but till seventy times seven times." And that does not mean four hundred and ninety—that means infinity.

Developing the idea of infinite mercy, Our Lord said he had come "to heal the contrite of heart"; and that "they that are in health need not a physician, but they that are ill....For I am not come to call the just, but sinners."

Some were scandalized at him because he "dined with publicans and sinners," but he never ceased to remind us that we should be merciful because the heavenly Father was merciful. "That you may be the children of your Father who is in heaven, who makes his sun to rise upon the good and bad, and rains upon the just and the unjust. For if you love them that love you, what reward shall you have? Do not even the publicans do this?...Be you therefore perfect as also your heavenly Father is perfect."

Here he is suggesting that we must, like Our Heavenly Father, be merciful to those who, according to human estimation, least deserve it. That is why he was merciful to Magdalen, to the woman at the well, to Peter who denied him, to Zacchaeus, and even to Judas whom he addressed as "friend."

There was no mistaking his point of view; he was interested in sinners not because of their merits, but because of their misery. And now at the close of his life, he fulfills the Beatitude of Mercy in his second word from the Cross.

There were three crosses on Calvary: the crosses of two thieves and the Cross of the Good Shepherd. Of the three who hung silhouetted against that blackened sky, one was selfish and thought only of himself—that was the thief on the left. He was interested neither in the Savior who suffered patiently nor in the thief who begged for mercy. He had no thought but for himself as he addressed the Man on the central cross: "If you be Christ, save yourself and us."

The thief on the right, on the contrary, thought not of himself, but about others, namely the thief on the left and Our Blessed Lord. His compassion went out to the thief on the left, because he was not turning to God in this the last hour of his life and begging for forgiveness: "Neither do you fear God, seeing you are under the same condemnation." He also thought of the meek Man crucified between the two of them, who had just prayed for his executioners and was innocent and good: "We indeed (suffer) justly, for we receive the due reward of our deeds; but this man has done no evil."

It is interesting to inquire why the merciful Savior not only forgave the penitent thief, but even gave him the Divine Promise: "This day you shall be with me in paradise." Why did not Our Lord address the same words to the thief on the left? The answer is to be found in the Beatitude of Mercy: "Blessed are the merciful: for they shall obtain mercy."

Because the thief on the right was merciful and compassionate, he received mercy and compassion. Because he was thoughtless of self, someone thought of him. There is a law about mercy just as rigid as the laws of nature. What we sow that also we reap. If we sow sparingly we reap sparingly. If we sow generously we reap an abundant harvest. Raised to a spiritual level, this means, as Our Lord has said, "For with what judgment you judge, you shall be judged; and with what measure you mete, it shall be measured to you again."

In other words, by thinking of others we get God to think of us. If the seed of the springtime thought only of self, but never of the soil, the rain, and the sun, it would never bloom and blossom into flower and fruit. But once it forgets itself and goes outside itself, and even dies to seed-life for the sake of the soil and sun and air, lo! it finds itself renewed and beautified a thousand times. If the coal in the bowels of the earth thought only of itself, it would never release its imprisoned sunlight as light and heat.

And so it is with us. Mercy is a compassion that seeks to unburden the sorrows of others as if they were our own. But if we have no such compassion, then how can compassion ever come back to us?

Unless we throw something up, nothing will come down; unless there is an action there can never be a reaction; unless we give, it shall not be given to us; unless we love, we shall not be loved; unless we pardon evil, our evil shall not be forgiven; unless we are merciful to others, God cannot be merciful to us.

If our heart is filled with the sand of our ego, how can God fill it with the fire of his Sacred Heart? If there is no "for sale" sign on the selfishness of our souls, how can God take possession of them?

If then we wish to receive mercy, we must, like the good thief, think of others, for it seems that God finds us best when we are lost in others. *Blessed are the merciful; for they shall obtain mercy.*

In a negative way, Our Lord has reminded us of this Law of Mercy in the parable of the unjust steward:

> Therefore is the kingdom of heaven likened to a king, who would take an account of his servants. And when he had begun to take the account, one was brought to him that owed him ten thousand talents. And as he had not wherewith to pay it, his lord commanded that he should be sold, and his wife and children, and all that he had, and payment to be made. But that servant falling down, besought him, saying: "Have patience with me, and I will pay thee all." And the lord of that servant, being moved with pity, let him go and forgave him the debt.
>
> But when that servant was gone out, he found one of his fellow-servants that owed him a hundred pence: and laying hold of him, he throttled him, saying: "Pay what thou owest." And his fellow-servant falling down, besought him, say-

ing: "Have patience with me, and I will pay you all." And he would not, but went and cast him into prison, till he paid the debt.

Now his fellow-servants, seeing what was done, were very much grieved, and they came, and told their lord all that was done. Then his lord called him and said to him: "You wicked servant, I forgave you all the debt, because you beseeched me. Should not you then have had compassion also on thy fellow-servant, even as *I* had compassion on you?" And his lord being angry, delivered him to the torturers until he paid all the debt. So also shall my heavenly Father do to you, if you forgive not every other brother from your hearts.

Be merciful then to others, if you would have God be kind to you at the last day. Think of others, rather than of yourself. Our Lord has made mercy the very soul of his Church. I think that is the reason why he chose as the head of his Church, not the innocent, not the pure, not the virgin disciple John, but that impetuous, strong man called Peter—the one who had denied him, and who, the night of the trial, cursed and swore that he knew not the Man. His merciful Lord passed him en route to the ignominy of that sorrowful night preceding Good Friday, and Peter, seeing him, went out and "wept bitterly." And tradition adds that Peter wept so much during his life that even his cheeks became furrowed with tears.

And so he who knew by experience the mercy and for-giveness of Our Lord was chosen the head of the Church, in order that the Church might forever practice mercy and kindness.

There is every reason in the world for mercy. There is some good in the worst of us, and there is some bad in the best of us. The good are those who try to find some good in others, and they generally do find it. The evil are those who look for the faults of others, and as a result never see their own. It was these Our Lord rebuked: "And why do you see the mote that is in your brother's eye, and do not see the beam that is in your own eye? Or how say you to your brother: Let me cast the mote out of your eye; and behold a beam is in your own eye! You hypo-crite, cast out first the beam of your own eye, and then shall you see to cast out the mote of your brother's eye."

If then on the last day we would receive a merciful judgment, we must begin here on earth to be merciful to others. Just as the clouds release only the moisture which they gathered from the earth, so too can Heaven release only the mercy we have sent heavenward.

By constantly thinking of ourselves, we render ourselves incapable of receiving the kindness of others. Only to the extent that we have emptied ourselves of ourselves can God fill us with himself. And likewise, the best way to have our prayers answered is to pray for the intentions of others: for God begins to think of us when we cease to think of ourselves.

Therein probably lies the reason why more of our prayers are not answered. How can God answer the prayers we address to him unless we answer the prayers others address to us? Do we answer the prayers of the poor? the maimed? the lame? the sinner? the missionary? If not, then by what right can we expect God to answer our requests? How can God give us his gifts, if we never give others our gifts? How can God fill our coffers with his treasures, unless we empty them to others?

The law is as simple as that: sow and you reap; do not keep your seed in your barns; give it away—scatter it over the fields; do the foolish thing; dissipate it, so that even the birds may eat of your bounty. And lo! in a short time you will find your seed increased five, ten, one hundredfold. But keep it in your barn, and the birds starve and you have no increase.

Give and you shall receive; be merciful and you shall receive mercy. When therefore you are on a cross of pain or sorrow always think of that cross as the cross of the thief on the right.

As such, let your prayers go out to those on the left cross that they may be mindful of the expiatory value of their suffering; let your love also go out to the Good Shepherd on the central Cross who suffers so innocently for all people, and because you never once thought of yourself but of others, or in other words, because you were merciful, you will hear the reward of mercy from the central Cross: "This day you shall be with me in paradise."

In that way you become another Good Thief, for a Good Thief is one who steals Paradise!

❀

If mercy were a sin, I believe I could
not keep from committing it.
—SAINT BERNARD OF CLAIRVAUX

Can it be a dream, that in the end man will find
his joy only in deeds of light and mercy,
and not in cruel pleasures as now…?
I firmly believe that it is not
and that the time is at hand.
People laugh and ask: "When will that time
come and does it look like coming?"
I believe that with Christ's help we shall
accomplish this great thing….
So it will be with us, and our people will shine
forth in the world, and all men will say:
"The stone which the builders rejected has become
the cornerstone of the building."
—DOSTOEVSKY, *BROTHERS KARAMAZOV*

CHAPTER THREE

❁

The Third Word:
The Lesson
of Purity

*Blessed are the
clean of heart:
for they shall see God.*

*(Son) behold your mother,
Woman, behold your son.*

On the Hill of the Beatitudes, at the beginning of his public life, Our Lord preached: "Blessed are the clean of heart, for they shall see God." Now at the end of his life, on the Hill of Calvary, he speaks to the clean of heart: "(Son) behold your mother, Woman, behold your son."

This, of course, is not the beatitude of the world. The world is living today in what might be described as an era of carnality, which glorifies sex, hates restraint, identifies purity with coldness, innocence with ignorance, and turns men and women into some sort of gods with their eyes closed, hands folded across their breasts, intently looking inward, thinking only of self.

It is just precisely against such a glorification of sex, and such egocentrism which is so characteristic of the flesh, that Our Lord reacted in his third Beatitude: "Blessed are the clean of heart."

The Third Beatitude and the Third Word are related as theory to practice and as doctrine to example, for it was the purity of Our Lord that made the gift of his Mother possible. This is the one supreme lesson to be drawn from this word, namely, that Mary became Our Mother because her Divine Son was purity itself. On no other condition could he have given her to us so completely and wholeheartedly.

In order to understand how Mary became Our Mother through purity, dwell for a moment on the nature of flesh.

Flesh is essentially selfish even in its legitimate satisfaction. All its pleasures look to itself and not to another. Even the law of self-preservation implies, as the word itself states, a kind of selfishness. In its illegitimate pursuits, flesh is even more selfish still, for to satisfy itself it must tyrannize over others, and consume them to enkindle its own fires.

But God in his wisdom has instituted two escapes from the selfishness of the flesh: the sacrament of matrimony and the vow of chastity. Each not only breaks the circle of selfishness but makes possible a greater and wider field of service. Or to turn the truth around: the greater the purity of heart, the less the selfishness.

The first escape from the selfishness of the flesh, which God has instituted, is the sacrament of matrimony. Matrimony crushes selfishness, first of all, because it merges individuals into a corporate life in which neither lives for self but for the other; it crushes selfishness also because the very permanence of marriage is destructive of those fleeting infatuations, which are born with the moment and die with it; it destroys selfishness, furthermore, because the mutual love of husband and wife takes them out of themselves into the incarnation of their mutual love, their other selves, their children; and finally it narrows selfishness because the rearing of children demands sacrifice, without which, like unwatered flowers, they wilt and die.

But these are only negative aspects of matrimony in

relation to the flesh. What is more important to note is that matrimony cures selfishness by calling the flesh to the service of others. New horizons and vistas of devotion and sacrifice are opened to the eyes of flesh; others become more important than self; the ego becomes less circumscribed and more expansive. If reaches out to others, at times even forgetting self.

And so true is this that there is generally less selfishness in large families than in small ones. A husband and wife may live only for each other, but a father and mother must die to themselves in order to live for their offspring. All unregulated and egotistic attachments that destroy the integrity of a common life are left behind them. Where their heart is, there is their treasure also. They lay their flesh on the altar of sacrifice that others may live, and this is the beginning of love.

But God has provided still another escape from the selfishness of flesh, one more complete than the sacrament of matrimony, and that is the vow of chastity. The man or woman who takes this vow does so, not to escape the sacrifices that marriage demands, but to detach himself from all the ties of the flesh, in order that he may be free for greater service.

As Saint Paul puts it: "He that is with a wife is solicitous for the things of the world, how he may please his wife; and he is divided. He that is without a wife is solicitous for the things that belong to the Lord, how he may please God."

The vow is a higher form of sacrifice than matrimony, simply because it purchases greater release from the claims of the flesh. The greater the purity the less the selfishness. He or she who takes it may be free to serve and love not just another man or woman and a few children, but all men and all women and all children in the bonds of charity in Christ Jesus Our Lord.

Marriage releases the flesh from its individual selfishness for the service of the family; the vow of chastity releases the flesh not only from the narrow and circumscribed family where there can still be selfishness, but also for the service of that family which embraces all humanity. That is why the Church asks those who consecrate themselves to the redemption of the world to take a vow and to surrender all selfishness, that they may belong to no one family and yet belong to all.

That is why in that larger family of the Kingdom of God, the priest is called "Father"—because he has begotten children not in the flesh, but in the Spirit. That is why the superior of a religious community of women is called "Mother"—she has her little flock in Christ. That too is why certain teaching orders of men are called "Brothers," and why women bound in religious life by the vow of chastity are called "Sisters."

They are all one family in which new relations have been established, not by their birth in the flesh but by their birth in Christ—all selflessly seeking the glory of God and the salvation of sinners, under the one whom they love most on earth: their Holy Father, the successor of Peter, the Vicar of Jesus Christ.

Now if matrimony and the vow of chastity provide releases from the selfishness of the flesh, and if increasing purity prepares for a wider service of others, then what should we expect when we meet perfect purity?

If a person becomes less and less egocentric as he becomes more pure, then what should we look for in perfect sinlessness and perfect purity? If greater purity means greater selflessness, then what should we expect of innocence? The answer is: perfect sacrifice.

Given a character in whom there is no selfishness, either for his own comfort or even for his own life, and you have the sacrifice of the Cross. "For greater love than this no man has, that a man lay down his life for his friends." Given a purity that rises above all family ties and bonds of blood, and then, as Our Lord told us: "He that does the will of the Father in heaven is a father, a mother, a brother, and a sister."

Given a purity that is the purity of Our Lord on the Cross, and you have someone so detached from the ego, so strange to selfishness, so thoughtless of the flesh that he looks upon his Mother, not uniquely as his own, but as the Mother of us all. Perfect purity is perfect selflessness. That is why Christ gives his Mother to us, as represented in the person of John: "Behold your mother."

He would not be selfish about her; he would not keep just for himself the loveliest and most beautiful of all mothers; he would share his own mother with us: and so at the foot of the Cross he gave her who is the Mother of God to us as the mother of men. No human person could do that because the ties of flesh and the selfishness of the flesh are too close. The flesh is too close to us to enable us to share our mother with others. But absolute purity can.

That is why the Beatitude of Purity is one with the Third Word, where selflessness, reaching its perfection in purity, gave his life that we might be saved, and gave us his Mother that we might not be orphans.

Purity, then, is not something negative; it is not just an unopened bud; it is not something cold; it is not ignorance of life. Is justice merely the absence of dishonesty? Is mercy merely the absence of cruelty? Is faith merely the absence of doubt? Purity is not merely the absence of sensuality; it is selflessness born of love and the highest love of all.

Everyone with a vow is in love, not in love with that which dies, but with that love which is eternal—the love of God. There is a passion about chastity—what Francis Thompson calls a "passionless passion and wild tranquillity."

Chastity is not an impossible virtue. Even those who have it not, may yet possess it. Saint Augustine calls Mary Magdalen "the arch-virgin." Think of it! the "arch-virgin." He puts her next to the Blessed Mother in virginity; Magdalen, this common prostitute of the streets! She recovered purity, we might almost say, by receiving in anticipation of the Eucharist, the night she bathed the feet of Our Lord with her tears. That day she came in contact with purity, and she so lived out its implications that within a short time we find her at the foot of the Cross on Good Friday. But who stands beside her? It is no other than the Blessed Mother.

What a remarkable companionship! A woman whose name a few months ago was synonymous with sin, and the Blessed Virgin! If Mary loved Magdalen, then why cannot she love us? If there was hope for Magdalen, then there can be hope for us. If she recovered purity, then it can be recovered by us. But how, except through Mary, for why is she called Mother Most Pure except to make us pure?

Everyone can go to Mary, not only converted sinners like Magdalen, but holy virgins and good mothers, for she is both Virgin and Mother. Virginity alone seems to lack something. There is a natural incompleteness about it—a faculty unused. Motherhood alone seems to have lost something. There is something surrendered in motherhood. But in Mary there is "neither lack nor loss," says Sheila Kay Smith. There is virginity and motherhood—"springtime of eternal May."

Purity, then, is not selfishness; it is surrender, it is thoughtfulness of others, it is sacrifice. It can even reach a peak where the Mother of Jesus can become our mother. Away then with that false maxim of the world which tells us that love is blind. It cannot be blind. Our Lord says it is not blind. "Blessed are the clean of heart, for they shall see"—see even God. Mary, open our eyes!

❀

Purity is the power to contemplate defilement.
—SIMONE WEIL, *GRAVITY AND GRACE*

The impure then cannot love God; and those who are without love of God cannot really be pure. Purity prepares the soul for love, and love confirms the soul in purity.
—JOHN HENRY CARDINAL NEWMAN,
DISCOURSES TO MIXED CONGREGATIONS.

CHAPTER FOUR

❀

The Fourth Word: The Lesson of Poverty

*Blessed are the poor
in Spirit,
for theirs is the
kingdom of heaven.*

*My God, my God,
why have you
forsaken me?*

At the beginning of his public life on the Hill of the Beatitudes, Our Lord preached: "Blessed are the poor in Spirit, for theirs is the Kingdom of Heaven." At the end of his life on the Hill of Calvary, he now practices that poverty of Spirit by his Fourth Word from the Cross: "My God, my God, why have you forsaken me?"

Both the Beatitude and the Word are foreign to the spirit of the world. Modern society is what might be characterized as acquisitive, for its primary concern is to acquire, to own, to possess; its aristocracy is not one of blood or virtue, but of money; it judges worth not by righteousness but in terms of possessions.

Our Blessed Lord came into the world to destroy this acquisitiveness and this subservience of moral to economic ends by preaching the blessedness of the poor in Spirit. It is worth noting immediately that "the poor in spirit" does not necessarily mean the indigent or those in straitened circumstances of life. "Poor in spirit" means interior detachment, and as such includes even some who are rich in the world's goods, for detachment can be practiced by the rich just as avarice can be practiced by the poor.

The poor in Spirit are those who are so detached from wealth, from social position, and from earthly knowledge that, at the moment the Kingdom of God demands a sacrifice, they are prepared to surrender all.

The Beatitude means then: Blessed are those who are

not possessed by their possessions; blessed are they who whether or not they are poor in *fact* are poor in their inmost spirit.

Our Lord not only preached poverty of Spirit; he also lived it, and he lived it in such a way as to conquer the three kinds of pride: the pride of what one has, which is economic pride; the pride of what one is, which is social pride; and the pride of what one knows, which is intellectual pride.

First of all, to counteract the wild exaltation of the economic, the pursuit of wealth as the noblest end of man, and the glorying in what one has, Christ became economically poor. He chose his Mother from the poorer classes who could afford to offer only doves in the Temple, and his foster father from the village tradesmen; and he who owned the earth and the fullness thereof, chose for his birthplace a deserted shepherd's cave.

He was poor in his mission as he explained at Nazareth: "The Spirit of the Lord is upon me, wherefore he has anointed me to preach the gospel to the poor." He was poor in his public life: "The foxes have holes, and the birds of the air nests; but the Son of man has no where to lay his head."

He was poor in the eyes of government, for when asked to pay the tax, he had no money. He was poor in his death, for he was stripped of his garments—the last remnant of earthly possessions. He was executed on a cross erected at public expense, and buried in a stranger's grave.

Thus did he atone for those who are proud of what they have, by having nothing, and becoming the Universal Poor Man of the world. He who was rich became poor for our sakes that we might be rich, and he is therefore the only one in all history of whom both the rich and poor can say: "He came from our ranks. He is one of our own."

Reparation had to be made not only for the pride of wealth but also for the snobbery and pride of social position. The world is full of those who through either the accident of birth or circumstance count themselves better than their fellowmen and who glory in what they are.

These too he atoned for not only by veiling the glory of his Godhead under human form but also by the most poignant social abandonment. The very beginning of his life bears the record: "He came unto his own, and his own received him not." Cities abandoned him; Bethlehem refused him an inn; Nazareth drove him from its gates; and Jerusalem stoned him.

Truly indeed he could say: "A prophet is not without honor, but in his own country, and in his own house, and among his own kindred." Men abandoned him. Some of His disciples, upon hearing him say he would give himself humbly under the form of Bread, said: "This saying is hard, and who can hear it?"...and they walked with him no more.

Teachers of the Law abandoned him, calling him "a glutton, a wine-drinker, a friend of publicans and sinners." The needy abandoned him and drew from him the sweet complaint: "You will not come to me that you may have life." One of his apostles abandoned him for thirty pieces of silver, one for shame at the word of a maidservant, and three for sleep. Even those whom he helped abandoned him. "Were not ten made clean? and where are the other nine? There is no one found to return and give glory to God, but this stranger."

And now at the end of his life, the Roman governor could say: "Your own nation...has delivered you up to me." Thus did he who is King of Kings become socially poor and an outcast from the snobs of the earth, in order that through that abandonment we might become—let us pause at the very thought of it—*children of God*!

Finally, he atoned for the intellectually proud, for all those who think they know, and who rely on the sufficiency of human knowledge without faith, by becoming spiritually poor.

During his public life he rejoiced that the sublime truths of the Kingdom of Heaven were given only to the humble: "I confess to you, O Father, Lord of heaven and earth, because you have hid these things from the wise and prudent, and have revealed them to little ones."

The night of his agony in the garden when that atonement for pride began in all horror, he described his soul as "sorrowful unto death"; and now on the Cross he lives the Beatitude of the Poor in Spirit by proclaiming the last and greatest poverty of all—the spiritual poverty of seeming abandonment by God: "My God, my God, why have you forsaken me?"

Even the sun at midday hid its light as a symbol of the spiritual desolation of his soul. The Father had not really abandoned him, but Our Lord restrained his Divinity from mitigating even with one drop of consolation the bitterness of his chalice.

The cry was one of abandonment, not one of despair. A soul that despairs never cries to God. Just as the keenest pangs of hunger are felt not by the dying man who is completely exhausted, but by the man battling for his life with the last ounce of strength, so abandonment is felt not by the ungodly and unholy, but by the most holy of men, Our Lord on the Cross.

This was the hardest reparation of all. It was not difficult to be economically poor; it was not so difficult to be socially poor and stripped of his friends. But it was hard to surrender divine consolation in a moment of agony to atone for the self-wise, the intelligentsia, and the conceited who refuse to bow their heads to the wisdom of God, for the atheists who live without God, and for the godless who blot his name from the land of the living.

This word from the Cross was a revelation of how much mental agony there must be in the world in those minds and souls and hearts who are without God. Jesus knew at that one moment what it was to be without God! He knew something of the loneliness of godlessness and something of its misery, for it was the one moment in which he suffered the desolation of both, that we might have the consolation of never being without him. By feeling without God, he redeemed those who live without him.

Behold the Poor Man. Economically poor because stripped of garments; socially poor because deserted by friends; spiritually poor because abandoned by God. From that day to this, then: Blessed are the poor in Spirit. Blessed are the economically poor in spirit for, by desiring nothing, they possess all, even the mansions of the Father's House.

Some years ago when the cloister of a Carmelite convent was broken by a Cardinal and opened to the public, a good Carmelite nun was showing a visiting priest through the convent. From the roof of it one could look over a valley, and on to an opposite hill where there stood a large and beautiful home that seemed to stand as a symbol for all that was sweet and beautiful and lovely in life.

Recalling the economic poverty of this poor nun, the visitor said to her, "Sister, just suppose that before you entered Carmel, you could have lived in that home. Suppose that you could have had all the wealth, refinement, and opportunities for worldly enjoyment that such a home would give you. Would you have left that house to have become a poor Carmelite?" And she answered, "Father, that *is* my house!"

Blessed also are the poor in spirit socially. Blessed are they who know of only one aristocracy—the blue bloods born at the baptismal font and the royalty of the King of Kings.

There is going to be a tremendous transformation of social position at the last day, for God is no respecter of persons. Our social position in the Kingdom of God will depend not upon our human popularity or the popularity of propagandists, but only upon those things we carry with us in the shipwreck of the world—a clear conscience and the love of God.

The world has little use for either, that is why Our Lord warned us that a full-hearted love of him would draw down the world's hatred: "Yea, the hour comes, that whosoever kills you, will think that he does a service to God. And these things will they do to you, because they have not known the Father, nor me. But these things I have told you, that when the hour shall come, you may remember that I told you of them."

How completely his point of view reverses that of the world's estimate of position is evidenced in those equally striking words: "Blessed shall you be when men shall hate you, and when they shall separate you, and shall reproach you, and cast out your name as evil, for the Son of Man's sake. Be glad in that day and rejoice; for behold, your reward is great in heaven."

Blessed finally are the poor in spirit intellectually. Blessed are the humble, and the teachable who like the Shepherds know they know nothing, or like the Wise Men who know they do not know everything. Faith in God, faith in prayer, hope in Christ, devotion to Our Blessed Mother, belief in the Eucharist and in infallibility—all this may seem foolish to the self-wise, but "the foolishness of God is wiser than men."

Personally, we feel that if our eternal salvation were conditioned upon saving either one hundred corrupt men and women of the streets like Magdalen and Zacchaeus, or converting one proud university professor who felt his tiny mind had solved all the riddles of the universe, we should choose to go out and convert the hundred.

And there is a divine warrant for the choice, for Our Lord said to those who thought themselves wise: "Amen, I say to you, that the publicans and the harlots shall go into the Kingdom of God before you."

Why, then, are we proud? Why do we set all the energies of life on becoming rich: "What does it profit a man, if he gain the whole world, and suffer the loss of his own soul?" Why do we seek social prestige and seek out the first places at tables—the divine injunction is just the contrary: "When you are invited, go, sit down in the lowest place; that when he who invited you comes, he may say to you: Friend, go up higher....Because every one that exalts himself shall be humbled; and he that humbles himself shall be exalted."

Why are we proud? Whom in all the world could we find to love us in poverty, in friendless abandonment, and in ignorance, other than Our Lord? In the beautiful words of Francis Thompson:

Strange, piteous, futile thing!
Wherefore should any set thee love apart?
Seeing none but I make much of naught"
　　(He said),
And human love needs human meriting:
　　How hast thou merited—
Of all man's clotted clay, the dingiest clot?
　　Alack, thou knowest not
How little worthy of any love thou art!
Whom wilt thou find to love ignoble thee,
　　Save Me, save only Me?
All which I took from thee I did but take,
　　Not for thy harms,
But just that thou might'st seek it in My arms.
　　All which thy child's mistake
Fancies as lost, I have stored for thee at home:
　　Rise, clasp My hand, and come.

If then we are called to be poor economically, poor
socially, and poor intellectually, let us rejoice in the hope
that for us is reserved the Kingdom of Heaven, and for
the present see in our fleeting poverty "the shade of His
hand, outstretched caressingly."

Most of the luxuries, and many of the so-called
comforts of life, are not only not indispensable,
but positive hindrances to the elevation of mankind.
With respect to luxuries and comforts,
the wisest have ever lived a more simple
and meager life than the poor.
—THOREAU, *WALDEN*

Grant me the treasure of sublime poverty:
permit the distinctive sign of our order to be
that it does not possess anything of its
own beneath the sun, for the glory of
your name, and that it have no other
patrimony than begging.
—SAINT FRANCIS OF ASSISI,
QUOTED IN MAURICE KEEN,
A HISTORY OF MEDIEVAL EUROPE

CHAPTER FIVE

❊

The Fifth Word:
The Lesson
of Zeal

*Blessed are they
that hunger and thirst
after justice: for they shall
have their fill.*

I thirst.

At the beginning of his public life on the Hill of the Beatitudes, Our Lord preached the necessity of zeal: "Blessed are they that hunger and thirst after justice: for they shall have their fill." At the end of his public life on the Hill of Calvary he practiced that Beatitude as there fell from his lips the cry of apostleship: "I thirst."

The world cannot understand either this Beatitude or this Word, for the world by its nature is seated in indifference. It is very fond of talking about religion, but dislikes doing anything about it. It dismisses zeal and intense love of God with the sneer of "mysticism," and regards religion as something incidental to human life, like poetry.

It is not uncommon, therefore, to find Catholics who say: "I knew I should not eat meat on Friday out of respect for the day on which Our Lord sacrificed his life for me, but I did not want to embarrass my host," or "I was staying with some unbelieving friends over the weekend and I did not want to embarrass them, so I did not go to Mass on Sunday," or "When they made fun of devotion to the Blessed Mother and ridiculed veneration of saints, and the crucifix, I said nothing, because I did not want to start an argument about religion."

Such is the indifference of the world—a fear of being identified wholeheartedly with the God for whom we were made. If the world does hunger and thirst, it is always for something less than the justice of this Beatitude.

The godless, for example, hunger and thirst, but not for the justice of God; they hunger and thirst for a world system built, not upon love, but upon superiority of classes and upon revolutionary upheaval. They seek to fill a want, but only a material want.

It is just against such filling of the animal in us, and the starving of the spiritual, that Our Lord said: "Woe to you that are filled: for you shall hunger"; and "Your Father knows that you have need of all these things. Seek you therefore first the kingdom of God, and his justice, and all these things shall be added unto you."

And against that compromising indifference which fears to assert God's justice, he warned: "Everyone therefore that shall confess me before men, I will also confess him before my Father who is in heaven. But he that shall deny me before men, I will also deny him before my Father who is in heaven"; and against justice that limits itself to economic rights and excludes the duties of man to his Maker, he said: "For I tell you, that unless your justice abound more than that of the scribes and Pharisees, you shall not enter into the kingdom of heaven."

Not only negatively but positively did he preach the necessity of zeal for the justice of the Kingdom of God. His circumcision was a kind of impatience to run his course of justice which led to the Garden and the Cross; his teaching the Doctors in the Temple at twelve years of age was an impatience to teach others the sweetness of his Father's ways.

At the beginning of his public life we find him driving merchants out of the Temple, in fulfillment of the prophecy of apostleship: "The zeal of your house has eaten me up." Later on, he made use of a dinner invitation to save the soul of Magdalen, and on a hot day made use of a common love of cold water to bring the Samaritan woman to a knowledge of everlasting fountains. Jesus came, he said, "not to destroy souls, but to save"; and, "seeing the multitude, he had compassion on them; because they were distressed, and lying as sheep having no shepherd." Then he said to his disciples: "The harvest indeed is great, but the laborers are few. Pray you therefore the Lord of the harvest, that he send forth laborers into his harvest."

His whole mission in life was one of zeal, a hunger and thirst for the justice of God, which he perhaps best expressed in words of fire: "I am come to cast fire on the earth: and what do I will but that it be kindled? And I have a baptism wherewith I am to be baptized: and how am I straitened until it be accomplished!" Yet again, "And other sheep I have, that are not of this fold: them also I must bring, and they shall hear my voice, and there shall be one fold and one shepherd."

And now at the end of his life, he yearns still more for justice as he who called himself the Fountain of Living Waters and he who was figuratively the Rock that gave forth water as Moses struck it in the desert, now lets well from out his Sacred Heart the shepherd's call to all the souls of the world: "I thirst."

It was not a thirst for earthly waters, for the earth and its oceans were his. And when they offered him vinegar and gall as a sedative for his sufferings he refused it. It was therefore not a physical, but a spiritual thirst that troubled him—the thirst for the Beatitude of Justice—an insatiable thirst for the souls of human beings.

The world that dislikes zeal for God's justice, first hated it in him. It was his zeal that brought him to the Cross. The world loves the indifferent, the mediocre, the ordinary, but it hates two classes of people: those who are too good, and those who are too bad.

Hence, on Calvary we find Our Lord crucified with thieves. Both Innocence and Injustice fell foul of the law. Some go to the cross because they are too good for the majority or for the system; and others go to the cross because they are too bad for it.

The world hates the zealous, such as Our Lord, because they are a reproach to its mediocrity; it hates also the wicked, such as the thieves, because they are an annoyance to its self-complacency.

The race of quantity has always persecuted the race of quality. The good go down to death, because they are good; the wicked go to death because they are wicked—the mediocre survive. As Our Lord put it: "The world cannot hate you; but me it hates: because I give testimony of it, that the works thereof are evil." And if this was true of Our Lord, it must be true of us. The servant is not above the master.

If our passionate quest of God's cause makes us disliked by people, we cannot say we were not warned by him who was hated first. "If the world hate you, know you that it has hated me before you. If you had been of the world, the world would love its own: but because you are not of the world, but I have chosen you out of the world, therefore the world hates you....If they have persecuted me, they will also persecute you....That the word may be fulfilled which was written in their law: *They hated me without cause.*" Apostles of Christ, then, will never be popular. Their end is crucifixion.

And yet we must thirst for justice and be on fire for the Kingdom of God. Why? Because everything that is good diffuses itself. The sun is good, and it diffuses itself in light and heat; the flower is good, and it diffuses itself in perfume; the animal is good, and it diffuses itself in the generation of its kind; man is good, and he diffuses himself in the communication of thought; a Christian is good, and must therefore diffuse his Christianity, throw sparks from the flame of his love, enkindle fires in the inflammable hearts of others, and speak of his Lover because he is Love, for "out of the abundance of the heart the mouth speaks."

Strong love makes strong actions, and the measure of our zeal in bringing souls to the feet of Christ is the measure of our love of him.

Converting souls to Christ, then, is not based on the pride of propaganda and public relations, but on a desire for perfection. An apostle desires to bring men and women to Our Lord not for the same reason a business executive wishes to increase his trade.

The businessman advertises to increase his profits; the Christian propagandizes to increase the happiness of others. He wants to bring souls to Our Lord for the same reason he wants to see the sun shine, the flowers bloom, and lambs grow into sheep—because it is their perfection and therefore their happiness.

If a pencil is made for writing, we do not want to see it used for digging; if a bird is made for flying, we do not want to see it change places with the mole; if a soul is made for the fullness of life, then we do not want to see it clip its wings and wallow in hatred, half-truths, and marred loveliness. We want to see it united with its perfection which is the Life and Truth and Love and Beauty of God.

That is why a Christian soul is apostolic—it loves perfection, wholeness, completeness, happiness: God. And therefore it wants everyone to be God-like and God-ward.

And no cost is too great to achieve that end, for as Saint Paul writes:

Who then shall separate us from the love of Christ? Shall tribulation? or distress? or famine? or nakedness? or danger? or persecution? or the sword? (As it is written: *For your sake we are put to death all the day long. We are accounted as sheep for the slaughter.*) But in all these things we overcome, because of him that has loved us. For I am sure that neither death, nor life, nor angels, nor principalities, nor powers, nor things present, nor things to come, nor might, nor height, nor depth, nor any other creature shall be able to separate us from the love of God, which is in Christ Jesus Our Lord.

If there be hate, enmity, jealousy, and war on the face of the earth today, is it not due in the last analysis to our want of zeal for the cause of God?

Just suppose that outside of the necessary structure of the Church, there was only one in all the world who believed in it, who received Communion, acknowledged the primacy of Peter, and assisted at Holy Mass. Just suppose that that one zealous believer the first year converted one unbeliever to Christ and his Church. Suppose that the next year these two each made a convert; then there would be four the second year. And suppose the next year, these four made one apiece next year, then there would be eight converts at the end of the third year.

Now how many would there be, from that one zealous believer, at the end of only thirty years? There would be in the communion lines of the church at the end of the thirtieth year, one billion, seventy-three million, seven hundred and forty-one thousand, eight hundred and twenty-four souls breaking their fast with the Bread of Life.

It is a tremendous thought, and a reminder of how much we have failed to do our duty and to spread the love and knowledge of Christ in the souls of other people. Are we unmindful that thirst for justice will save our own souls? Have we forgotten the words of Saint James: "He who causes a sinner to be converted from the error of his way, shall save his soul from death, and shall cover a multitude of sins."

Have we forgotten that the cold must burn, that the tepid must flame like torches of the night, that the Kingdom of Heaven suffers violence and only the violent shall bear it away? If we have, then we know why Our Lord cried: "I thirst." It is because we have extended to him the vinegar and gall of indifference.

Away with mediocrity! Lift up your hearts! The world is looking for light. Will you hide yours under bushels? The earth is looking for savor, will you let the salt lose its savor? Think of those Communists who are hungering for justice without knowing it! Think of atheists, of the violent, of all who are starving for peace without knowing it! Think of the great mass of men and women in this country who set for themselves no higher a life than that of animals, namely, to eat and drink, sleep and search for prey.

Think of those who hate the good, really because they hate their own wickedness! They have a passion for God hidden beneath the ashes of their lives, but they presently live in fear "lest having Him they must have naught else besides."

We plead particularly for all those who hate religion, for those who hate their fellowman, and for those who hate God. But that does not mean we must hate them.

They are yearning for something that their own philosophy cannot give them. They are hungering and thirsting for the justice of God, whether they know it or not. Therefore we must not hate them just because they hate us. Rather, we must feel sorry for them because they miss so much, and because their zeal is bent on destruction rather than construction.

In fact, our sympathy for them should be so deep that we will strive to save them from the very ruins which, Samson-like, they pull down on their heads. This is our Christian duty, for we do not save our souls alone, but only in companionship with others.

On Judgment Day we shall be asked: Where are your children? If we can point to those whom we have saved, or can point to one whom we have made a Communionist, then we who hungered and thirsted shall be filled—filled even from the fountains of God.

Zeal without knowledge is
fire without light.
—THOMAS FULLER, *GNOMOLOGIA*

Had I but serv'd my God
with half the zeal I serv'd my king, he
would not in mine age Have left
me naked to mine enemies.
—WILLIAM SHAKESPEARE,
HENRY VIII, ACT 3, SCENE 2

❀

CHAPTER SIX

The Sixth Word: The Lesson of Peace

Blessed are the
peacemakers:
for they shall be called
the children
of God.

It is consummated.

At the beginning of his public life on the Hill of the Beatitudes, Our Lord preached: "Blessed are the peacemakers: for they shall be called the children of God." At the end of his life on the Hill of Calvary, he practiced that Beatitude as, concluding peace between man and God, he uttered the triumphant cry: "It is consummated."

Like all the other Beatitudes, this was at utter variance with the spirit of the world, where right is might, and where pugnacity and aggressiveness are virtues. This is putting it mildly, for in our generation there has arisen a philosophy of life whose first principle is dominance and superiority of one person or group over the other.

Never before in the history of the world did any political system profess, and much less act on, the motive of hate. We have it now in a world filled with political strife, which has almost drowned out the voice of the Prince of Peace.

But what is the peace spoken of in this Beatitude? The most perfect definition of peace ever given was that of Saint Augustine: *"Peace is the tranquillity of order."* It is not tranquillity alone, for some nations and peoples are tranquil through fear. Rather, it is the tranquillity of order in which there is no oppression from without, but rather a subordination of all things to the sovereign good which is God. Therefore the subjection of senses to reason, reason to faith, and the whole man to God as his eternal end and final perfection—that is the basis of peace.

It was just such a tranquillity of order which Our Lord brought to earth as the angels sang at his birth: "Glory to God in the highest, and on earth peace to men of good will." He bade his disciples to have peace with one another. Into whatsoever house they entered, they were first to say: "Peace be to this house."

The very Beatitude we are considering is a blessing on such peacemakers, and his words over Jerusalem a reminder of his sorrow at those who loved not peace: "If you also had known, and that in this your day, the things that are to your peace; but now they are hidden from your eyes."

The night of his arrest in the garden, when Peter drew his sword and cut off the right ear of the servant of the high priest, Our Lord rebuked him saying: "Put up again the sword into its place: for all that take the sword shall perish with the sword." Touching the ear of the wounded servant he made it whole.

The next afternoon, he who came to preach peace was put to death in the first world war of man against his Redeemer; but before he died Jesus pronounced the last and final words of peace: "It is finished."

What is finished? War is finished! The war against sin! The war against evil! The war against God! The work of atonement, which is *at-one-ment* with God, was completed. He has finished his Father's decade of the sorrowful mysteries, and the glorious ones were now about to begin.

The last farthing was paid. The Treaty of Peace was signed: "Blessed are the peacemakers." And now that he has made peace he could cry in triumph: "It is finished." It was not just an armistice; it was victory; it was a consummation—something done that could not be undone—Peace with God.

Thus far we have spoken of peace which Our Lord brought to earth. Now we must consider a difficulty against it. If Christ is the Prince of Peace, and it they who take the sword perish with the sword, and if a kingdom divided against itself will be brought to desolation, and if the Resurrection greeting is *pax*, then how do we reconcile these other seemingly contradictory words of Our Lord: "Do not think that I came to send peace upon earth: I came not to send peace, but the sword"; and "Think you, that I am come to give peace on earth? I tell you, no; but separation. For there shall be from henceforth five in one house divided three against two, and two against three. The father shall be divided against the son, and the son against the father, the mother against the daughter, and the daughter against the mother, the mother-in-law against her daughter-in-law and the daughter-in-law against her mother-in-law"; and "He that has not, let him sell his coat and buy a sword."

The explanation of these apparent contradictions is to be found in the words he addressed to his apostles the night of the Last Supper in which he made an important distinction between two kinds of peace: "My peace I give unto you; *not as the world gives,* do I give unto you"; and "These things I have spoken to you, that *in me* you may have peace. *In the world* you shall have distress: but have confidence: I have overcome the world." There is a difference, then, between his Peace and the peace of the world.

It is evident from these words that Our Lord offers a peace and a consolation that he alone can confer, a peace that comes from the right ordering of conscience, from justice, charity, love of God and love of neighbor. And blessed are those peacemakers who continue to spread that message of peace, for they shall be called the children of God; that is, they shall be recognized as possessing a divine characteristic which shall stamp them as God-like.

But these very lovers of peace, who follow in his footsteps, who take up their crosses daily, who love him more than all the world, who surrender all to be completely his, who trust in the Providence that feeds the birds, who have the faith of little children, and who love Christ and therefore seek that *interior peace* of conscience that only Christ can give—they will by that *very fact* be hated by the world.

The poor in spirit will be hated by those who pursue self-interest; the meek will be opposed by the self-assertive; those who hunger and thirst after justice will be scorned by the indifferent; the merciful will be ridiculed by the unforgiving; the pure of heart will be the laughingstock of the Freudians. The world whose false peace is based on self-love will make war against those whose peace is based on conscience.

In that sense Our Lord brought the sword—we might say he even made war—war against war, war against self-ishness, war against sin, war against godlessness. And if his war against evil brought him to the Cross, then his followers who preach his peace must also expect to be crucified.

The son who enters the priesthood rather than business may be hated by his father; the daughter who enters the convent rather than the social whirl may be hated by her mother; and the mother-in-law who pleads for the sanctity of the marriage bond may be hated by the daughter-in-law; and the daughter-in-law who is received into the Church to enjoy the security of its truth and the life of its Eucharist may be hated by her mother in-law. This is the meaning of Our Lord's words about a house being divided against itself.

A young man goes to college. He could there join an Oriental sun cult, or become a Buddhist, or a Confucianist, or start a new religion of his own, and his parents would probably only remonstrate; but let him join the Church and there would be war!

Truly indeed: "I came not to bring peace but the sword"—but Our Lord encouragingly reminds that young man that the war against him is only temporary. "In the world you shall have distress; but have confidence: I have overcome the world."

Yes, the Prince of Peace brings war—war against a false peace, war against tranquillity without order. If there is anything in life of which we must beware it is the danger of a false peace. Our Lord could have made a false peace with the world.

Did not the very ones who put him to death ask him to make terms with them? Did they not shout up to the throne: "Come down from the cross and we will believe"; in other words, "Come down and make a false peace. You are too insistent in the rights of your heavenly Father. You are too uncompromising about sin. You are too intolerant about your divinity. Can you not see that your claim to be the Son of God and Redeemer of the world is upsetting the world? Did you not hear one of the judges say to you last night 'One man must die for the nation to keep peace'? Come down and we will have peace."

Yes, if he had come down, there would have been peace; but a false peace! Our Lord stayed on the Cross until it was finished. He would not compromise his divinity. He would not compromise obedience to his Father's will. He would not minimize the horror of sin.

And so he stayed on the cross making war against evil until the battle was over, like a dying soldier who feebly fights with ebbing strength until his cause is victorious. That is why he could cry at the end: "It is consummated."

So, too, we must beware of a false peace—the kind that promises a better opportunity, but which ends in the destruction of peace. Such is peace as the world gives it.

Because we refuse to accept that false peace, because we refuse to come down from our cross and join in *their* false peace based on injustice, we bring down upon our heads their violence and their hate. But we cannot expect the world to treat us differently than it treated Our Lord.

Peace for us means a right conscience, not a dictatorship of the powerful; it means the tranquillity of order, not the overthrow of a just society; it means loving our enemies, not despising them; it means something in the inside of a person's soul, not something external.

We must beware, then, of concluding a false peace, of selling the Savior for thirty pieces of silver because he does not make us rich; of denying him before others because of the ridicule of maidservants; of sleeping during hours of great need; and above all else, of stepping down from the Cross, even after two hours and fifty-nine minutes of the world's crucifixion.

We must be prepared to suffer scorn, if for no other reason than because we are peacemakers; we must ever be ready to be hated by the world, for Our Lord told us we would be hated because of him. We must stay until "it is finished," even though that staying makes our fellowmen hate us.

This life is not a victory; this life is a war, and *God hates peace in those who are destined for war!*

If there is truly peace on earth,
goodwill to men, it will be because of women
like Mother Teresa.
Peace is not something you wish for;
it's something you make,
something you do, something you are,
and something you give away!
—ROBERT FULGHUM

Since wars begin in the minds of men,
it is in the minds of men that the defense
of peace must be constructed.
—ARCHIBALD MACLEISH

❀

CHAPTER SEVEN

The Seventh Word:
The Lesson
of Mourning

*Blessed are they
that mourn;
for they
shall be comforted.*

*Father, into your hands
I commend my spirit.*

At the beginning of his public life on the Hill of the Beatitudes, Our Lord preached: "Blessed are they that mourn; for they shall be comforted." At the end of his public life on the Hill of Calvary, he found that blessed comfort: "Father, into your hands I commend my spirit."

Like all the other beatitudes, this Beatitude of Mourning is quite different from the beatitude of the world: "Eat, drink, and be merry, for tomorrow we die." The world never regards mourning as a blessing, but always as a curse. Laughter is the gold it is seeking, and sorrow is the enemy it flees.

The world can no more understand the Beatitude of Mourning than it can understand the Cross. In fact, the modern man steels himself even against the suffering of another by wearing the mask of indifference, quite unmindful that such a thickening of his spiritual skin, though it may sometimes protect him from sorrow, nevertheless shuts in his own morbidity until it festers and corrupts.

But it must not be thought that the beatitude of Our Lord is either a condemnation of laughter and joy or a glorification of sorrow and tears. Our Lord did not believe in a philosophy of tragedy any more than we do. As a matter of fact, he upbraided the Pharisees because they wore long faces and looked sad when they fasted, and his apostles summed up his life and Resurrection in the one word "Rejoice."

The difference between the beatitude of the world, "Laugh and the world laughs with you," and the beatitude of Our Lord, "Blessed are they that mourn," is not that the world brings laughter and Our Lord brings tears. It is not even a choice of having or not having sadness; it is rather a choice of where we shall put it: at the beginning or at the end. In other words, which comes first: laughter or tears?

Shall we place our joys in time or in eternity, for we cannot have them in both. Shall we laugh on earth, or laugh in heaven, for we cannot laugh in both. Shall we mourn before we die or after we die, for we cannot mourn in both. We cannot have our reward both in heaven and on earth.

That is why we believe one of the most tragic words in the life of Our Lord is the word he will say to the worldly at the end of time: "You have already had your reward."

Which of the two roads, then, shall we take: the royal road of the Cross, which leads to the Resurrection and Eternal Life, or the road of selfishness, which leads to Eternal Death? The first road is filled with thorns, but if we traverse it far enough, we find it ends in a bed of roses; the other road is filled with roses, but if we traverse it far enough, it ends in a bed of thorns.

But we cannot take both roads or make the best of both worlds, because we cannot love both God and Mammon, any more than we can be both alive and dead at the same time. No person can serve two masters: "Either he will hate the one, and love the other; or he will sustain the one, and despise the other."

If we save our life in this world, we lose it in the next; if we lose our life in this world, we save it in the next. If we sow in sin, we reap corruption; if we sow in truth, we reap life everlasting. But we cannot do both.

With which, then, shall we begin—the fast or the feast? This is the problem of the beatitudes. Our Lord begins with the fast and ends with the feast; the world begins with the feast and ends with want.

The contrast between these two philosophies is recorded on every page of the Gospel. Dives was rich on this earth, but he had not even a drop of cold water after his death; Lazarus was a beggar on earth, but he became a rich man in the bosom of Abraham. Therefore, in the words of Our Lord: "Woe to you that now laugh: for you shall mourn and weep"; and "Blessed are you that weep now, for you shall laugh."

It is not surprising, then, to find that Our Lord who came into such utter conflict with the evil of the world should be described as the "Man of Sorrows," and one "Who in the days of his flesh with a strong cry and tears, offering up prayers and supplications to him that was able to save him from death, was heard for his reverence."

There is no record in the Gospels that he ever laughed, though there are many records of his tears. He openly wept at the grave of his friend Lazarus. He wept over the city that was to kill him, and amidst tears glistening on that heavenly face bemoaned: "Jerusalem, Jerusalem, you that kill the prophets, and stone them that are sent unto you, how often would I have gathered together your children, as the hen gathers her chickens under her wings, and thou would not!"

And not a long time afterwards he wept tears of crimson in the garden, as the "desperate tides of the great world's anguish forced through the channels of a single heart." And finally on the Cross after three hours of blood-weeping he comes to the end of his mourning.

Tears and crucifixions are not final; they are only the momentary death that even the seed endures before it bursts into the bloom and blossom of life. Had not the Lord said: "Blessed are you that weep now, for you shall laugh." He had had his fast, now he would have the feast; He had worn the thorns, now he would have the diadem of gold; He had mourned, now he would rejoice.

And in fulfillment of the beatitude of mourning, he lets ring out over Golgotha's hills in a commanding voice the last word he ever uttered on this earth as a suffering man, and it was a word of joy and triumph: "Father, into your hands I commend my spirit." It was the word of one who is strong and vigorous. No one was taking his life away. He was laying it down of himself, and nowhere does Sacred Scripture say that he died.

Death was not coming to him; it was he who was going to it. Death did not open its portals to him; He unlocked them of himself, for he knew where he was going.

His last hour was not like the pushing out of a boat into a trackless sea bound for unknown lands and under starless skies. His goal was fixed. He knew where he was going. The exiled King was going back home; the Prodigal Son was returning to the Father's house; the Heavenly Planet that thirty-three years before started out on its orbit to illumine a world, now returns to salute him who sent him on his way; the Great Captain now goes back to his native land bearing the glorious scars of victory.

The sorrowful mysteries are over; now begin the glorious ones. Truly indeed, "Blessed are they that mourn, for they shall be comforted."

The sorrow of Our Lord is over. He who mourned is comforted. But how about us? Which beatitude are we going to follow? Are we going to take all our laughter here below, or save some of it for eternity? Are we going to flee the cross now, or are we going to embrace it? Are we going to plan our life so that at the end we can say: "Father, into your hands I commend my spirit." If we are, then we must mourn. But why must we mourn?

We must mourn, first of all, because the world will make us mourn if we follow the Redeemer's beatitudes. If we practice meekness, the world will try to provoke us to anger; if we are merciful, the world will accuse us of not being just; if we are clean of heart, the world will shout "prudes"; if we hunger and thirst after justice, we shall not succeed; if we are peacemakers, the world will say we are cowards; if we are poor in spirit, the world will look down upon us.

In a word, suffering naturally follows the Christian's conflict with the evil of this world. Because we have been taken out of the world, the world will hate us. The servant is not above the master; if it made him weep crimson tears, it will make us weep too.

That is the first reason, then, why we must mourn: Because we have chosen the Man of Sorrows. But "blessed are you when they shall revile you and persecute you, and speak all that is evil against you, untruly for my sake: Be glad and rejoice, for your reward is very great in heaven."

There is another reason why we should mourn, and that is because of the sorrow we caused Our Lord's Blessed Mother. We can never grieve enough for grieving her who is our Mother too. And we did make her suffer, for there is never a wicked deed done in the world, but that there is an innocent victim.

The repercussion of sin is enormous. We throw a stone into the sea, and it causes a ripple that disturbs even the most distant shore. Calvary had its innocent victim too— one who had no share in bringing Our Lord to the Cross, in fact the only one who could ever say: "I am innocent of the blood of this man"—that innocent victim was Mary.

What had she done to deserve the Seven Swords? What crimes had she committed to rob her of her Son? She had done nothing; but we have. We have sinned against her

Divine Son, we have sentenced him to the Cross; and in sinning against him we wounded her.

In fact, we thrust into her hands the greatest of all griefs, for she was not losing a brother, or a sister, or a father, or a mother, or even just a son—she was losing God. And what greater sorrow is there than this!

Finally, we should mourn for the greatest of all reasons, namely, because of what our sins have done to him. If we had been less proud, his crown of thorns would have been less piercing; if we had been less avaricious, the nails in the hands would have been less burning; if we had traveled less in the devious ways of sin, his feet would not have been so deeply dug with steel; if our speech had been less biting, his lips would have been less parched; if we had been less sinful, his agony would have been shorter; if we had loved more, he would have been hated less.

There is a personal equation between that Cross and us. Life with its rebellions, its injustices, its sins, all played a role in the Crucifixion. We can no more wash our hands of our guilt than Pilate could wash his as he held them up under a noonday sun and declared himself innocent.

It was not so much the Crucifixion that hurt and wounded, it was not Annas, it was not Caiphas, it was not the executioners, for "they knew not what they did"; it was not his enemies who caused his greatest sorrow: "If my enemies had done this, I could have borne it." It was us who grieved him most, for we know what we do—we have tasted his sweetmeats; we have broken Bread with him; we are his familiars. That is our sorrow—that he who came to heal the broken hearts had his own Heart broken by us.

But mourning is not despair. If we have crucified Christ, there is pardon: "Father, forgive them"; if we have pierced Mary's heart, there is pardon still: "Son, behold your mother"; if there are tears in our eyes, they shall be wiped away: "Blessed are they that mourn, for they shall be comforted."

Think not, then, that the Beatitude of Mourning means the enthronement of sorrow, for it ends in the triumphant flight into the Father's embrace. All of you, therefore, who for months and years have lain crucified on beds of pain, remember that an hour will come when you will be taken down from your cross, and the Savior shall look upon your hands and feet and sides to find there the imprint of his wounds which will be your passport to eternal joy; for being made like him in his death, you shall be made like him in his glory.

All you husbands, wives, brothers, and sisters who have been bereaved of loved ones, remember that the Good Shepherd has taken his sheep to the green pastures that you, like other sheep, might follow your beloved even to the arms of Love.

To you whose life is as a fountain of tears for sins, remember that just as baptismal water washed away your original sin, so your tears will wash away your actual sins, and a day will come when God himself will wipe them all away.

To you who have lost faith, who have fear of confession, who dread casting yourself at the feet of Our Lord for absolution, remember that even your fear and your sin is a mourning, for you are most miserable on the inside.

You have broken your own heart, but be not disturbed. Take it to the anvil of Calvary, and under the fires of Love it shall be mended into that wholeness where it will never sorrow again, because when God mends a heart, it loses its capacity to sorrow and can only rejoice.

To all you who mourn, he has said: "Blessed are you, for you shall be comforted." You have had your fast with Christ, now you shall have his feast. He has saved much for you; He kept something back when he was on earth. He has reserved it for those who have wept.

And that thing that he has kept for eternity, which will make your life's crucifixion seem as naught, which will make your eternity a blissful ecstatic passionless passion of love, which will be the ending of all beatitudes and the crown of all living, that thing which he has guardedly treasured for eternity, and which will make heaven heaven, will be—his smile!

If we could read the secret history of our enemies,
we should find in each man's life sorrow
and suffering enough to disarm all hostility.
—HENRY WADSWORTH LONGFELLOW,
DRIFTWOOD

It is a good thing to have a great sorrow.
Or should human beings allow Christ
to have died on the Cross for the
sake of their toothaches?
—ISAK DINSEN, *LAST TALES*

About the Author

Fulton J. Sheen (1895–1979), one of the most notable Catholic prelates of all time, was a gifted orator, writer, preacher, and educator. He earned a J.C.B. from Catholic University in Washington, D.C. (where he later taught philosophy), a Ph.D. from Louvain University in Belgium, an S.T.D. from the Angelicum in Rome, and other degrees, including numerous honorary degrees.

The author of scores of books in the areas of theology, philosophy, Christian living, and spirituality, Sheen is also fondly remembered as a master of the media. In addition to his radio broadcast, *Catholic Hour*, and the award-winning television series, *Life Is Worth Living*, he wrote regular weekly newspaper columns—syndicated in both the religious and secular press—for more than two decades.